OXFORD
UNIVERSITY PRESS

Cello Time Christmas

piano accompaniment book

Kathy and David Blackwell

Great Clarendon Street, Oxford OX2 6DP, England

Oxford University Press is a department of the University of Oxford.
It furthers the University's aim of excellence in research, scholarship,
and education by publishing worldwide

Oxford is a registered trade mark of Oxford University Press
in the UK and in certain other countries

ISBN 978-0-19-337225-2

Music and text origination by
Barnes Music Engraving Ltd, East Sussex
Printed in Great Britain on acid-free paper by
Caligraving Ltd, Thetford, Norfolk.

Teacher's note

In Nos. 3, 7, 8, 15, 16, and 17, sections that are presented as repeats in the cello book are written out in the accompaniment.

Contents

4

1. Hark! the herald-angels sing

Felix Mendelssohn (1809–47)

Joyfully ♩ = 84

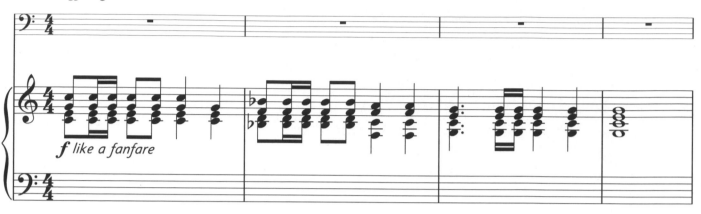

Hark! the he - rald - an - gels sing— Glo - ry to the new - born King;

Peace on earth and mer - cy mild,— God and sin - ners re - con - ciled:

Joy - ful all ye na - tions rise,_____ Join the tri - umph

of the skies,_____ With th'an - gel - ic host pro - claim,

Christ is_____ born in Beth - le - hem. Hark! the he - rald -

- an - gels sing Glo - ry_____ to the new - born King.

2. The holly and the ivy

English trad.

Flowing ♩ = 84

The hol - ly and the i - vy When they are both full

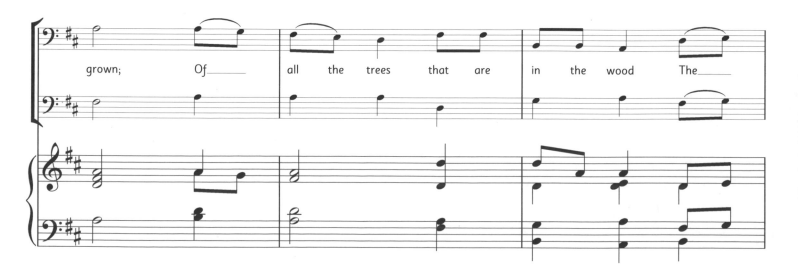

grown; Of___ all the trees that are in the wood The___

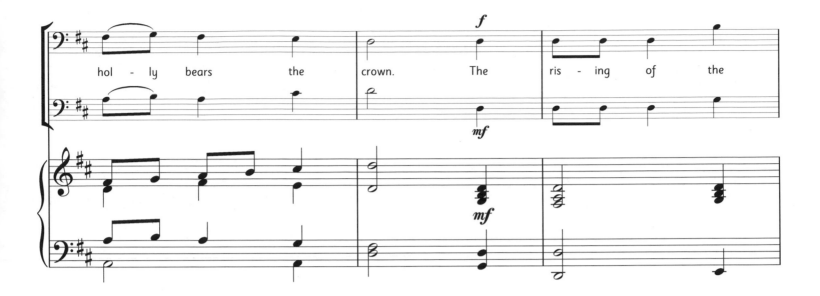

hol - ly bears the crown. The ris - ing of the

sun_____ And the run - ning of the deer, The_____

play - ing of the mer - ry or - gan, Sweet sing - ing in the choir.

3. Ding dong! merrily on high

16th-century French melody

Cheerfully ♩ = 100

Ding dong! mer - ri - ly on high in heav'n the bells are ring - ing:

Ding dong! ve - ri - ly the sky is riv'n with an - gel sing - ing.

Glo - - - - - - - - - - - -

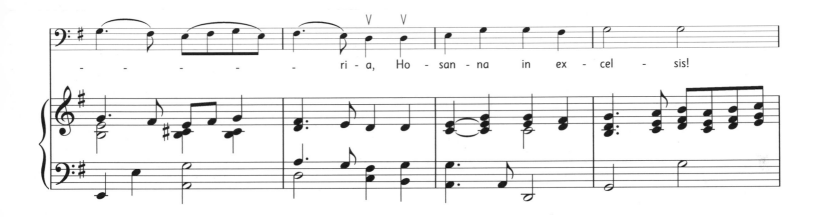

- - - - - ri - a, Ho - san - na in ex - cel - sis!

Glo - - - - - - - - - - -

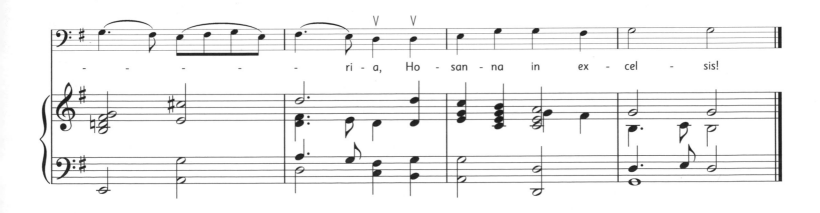

- - - - - ri - a, Ho - san - na in ex - cel - sis!

4. Andrew mine, Jasper mine

Simply ♩ = 66

Moravian carol

5. Silent night
next page

6. I saw three ships

English trad.

Nos. 5 and 6 have been reversed to avoid a page turn.

5. Silent night

Franz Gruber (1787–1863)

Tenderly ♩ = 88

mp legato

Ped.

mp

Si - lent night, ho - ly night,

_∧ *etc.*

All is calm, all is bright;

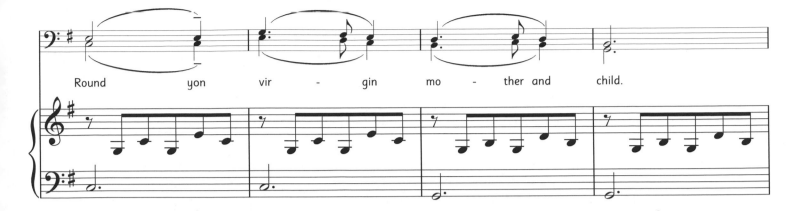

Round yon vir - gin mo - ther and child.

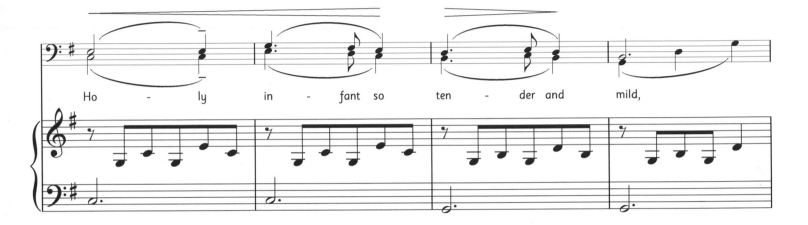

Ho - ly in - fant so ten - der and mild,

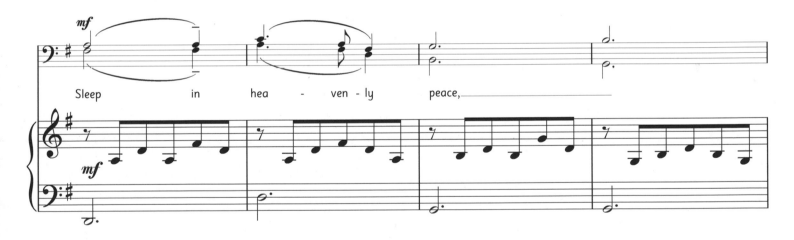

Sleep in hea - ven - ly peace,

Sleep in hea - ven - ly peace.

7. O little town of Bethlehem

English trad.

8. Once in royal David's city

H. J. Gauntlett (1805–76)

Once in ro - yal Da - vid's ci - ty Stood a low - ly cat - tle shed, Where a mo - ther laid her ba - by in a man - ger for his bed: Ma - ry was that mo - ther mild, Je - sus Christ her lit - tle child.

9. Go tell it on the mountain

With energy ♩ = 96

American trad.

Go tell it on the moun - tain,

Fine

o - ver the hills and ev - 'ry - where; Go tell it on the moun - tain that Je - sus Christ is born!

Shep - herds kept their watch - ing o'er wand - 'ring flocks by night; Be -

D.%. al Fine

- hold from out of hea - ven there shone a ho - ly light:_____

10. We wish you a merry Christmas

trad. West Country

Cheerfully ♩ = 90 (jazz waltz, straight 8s)

mf

con Ped.

We wish you a mer-ry

Christ-mas, We wish you a mer-ry Christ-mas, We wish you a mer-ry Christ-mas And a

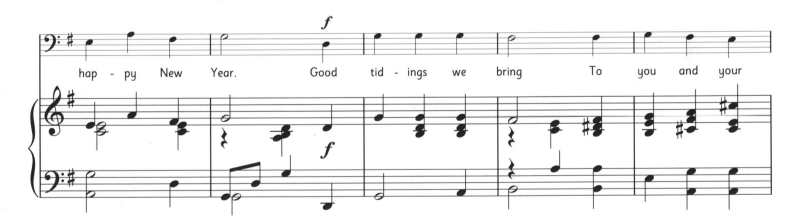

f

hap-py New Year. Good tid-ings we bring To you and your

kin; We wish you a mer-ry Christ-mas And a hap-py New Year.

11. Shepherds watched

Czech carol

Shep - herds watched their lambs and sheep,

Through the night so dark and deep. Lo, the an - gel in the skies, Bid - ding them to stand and rise.

Hi - dom, hi - dom, hi - do - dom, Hi - dom, hi - dom, hi - do - dom.

Hi - dom, hi - dom, hi - do - dom, Hi - dom, hi - dom, hi - do - dom.

12. O Christmas tree

German trad.

13. We three kings

J. H. Hopkins (1820–91)

Stately ♩ = 98

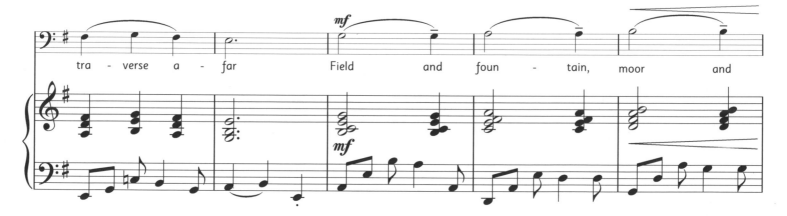

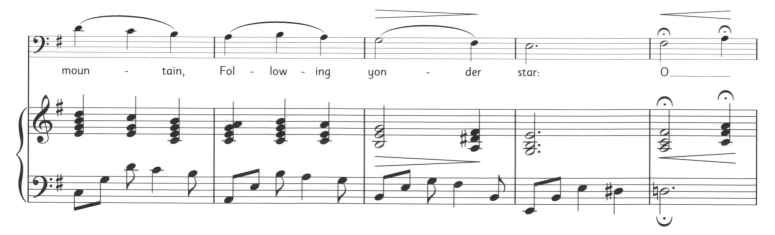

mp mysteriously

We three kings of O - ri - ent are; Bear - ing gifts we tra - verse a - far Field and foun - tain, moor and moun - tain, Fol - low - ing yon - der star: O

star of won - der, star of night,

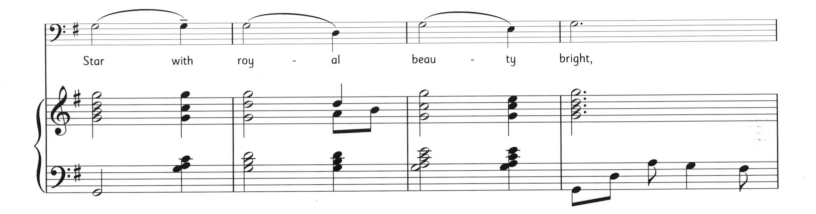

Star with roy - al beau - ty bright,

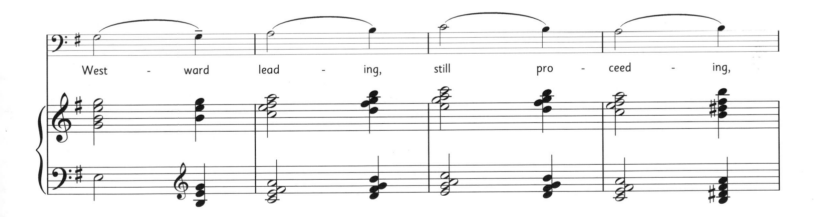

West - ward lead - ing, still pro - ceed - ing,

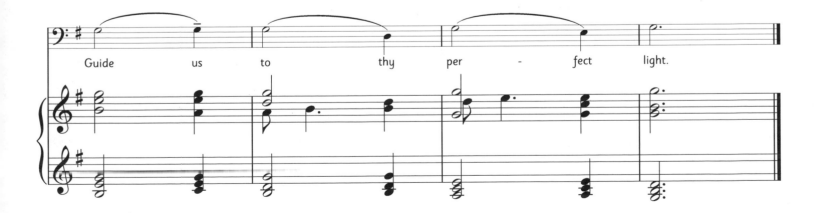

Guide us to thy per - fect light.

14. Bethl'em lay a-sleeping

Polish carol

15. Good King Wenceslas

Piae Cantiones (1582)

16. Infant holy, infant lowly

Polish carol

Like a lullaby ♩ = 64

17. Deck the hall

Welsh trad.

Lively ♩ = 90

18. O come, all ye faithful

J. F. Wade (*c.*1711–86)

Come and be - hold him Born the King of An - gels: O

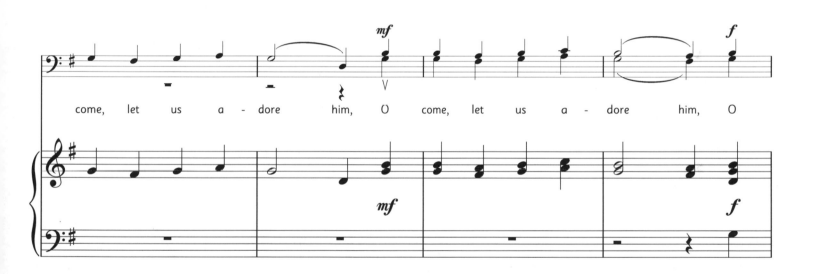

come, let us a - dore him, O come, let us a - dore him, O

come, let us a - dore him,_____ Christ_____ the Lord!

19. Away in a manger

William J. Kirkpatrick (1838–1921)

Tenderly ♩ = 68

20. The first Nowell

English trad.

21. Zither Carol

Czech carol

Brightly ♩ = 80

Girls and boys, leave your toys, make no noise, Kneel at his crib and wor-ship him. At thy shrine, child di - vine, we are thine, Our Sa - viour's here. 'Hal - le - lu - jah' the church bells ring, 'Hal - le - lu - jah' the an - gels sing, 'Hal - le - lu - jah' from ev - 'ry - thing. All must draw near.

22. God rest you merry, gentlemen

English trad.

23. Skaters' Waltz

Emil Waldteufel (1837–1915)

Cello parts swap round on repeat. In the cello book the repeat is written out.

24. Dance of the Reed Pipes

(from the *Nutcracker* ballet)

Pyotr Ilyich Tchaikovsky (1840–93)

Andante ♩ = 90

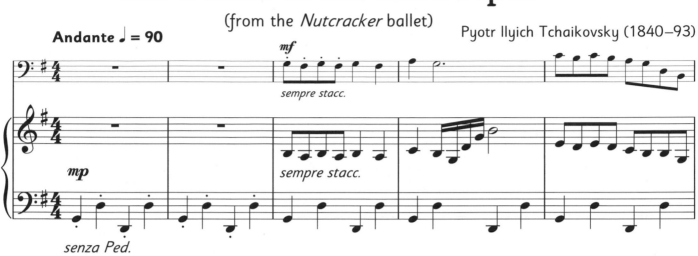

25. While shepherds watched their flocks

Este's Psalter (1592)

26. Children, go!

27. Child in a manger

Celtic trad.

Lyrics:
Child in a man - ger, Je - sus our Sa - viour, Born of a vir - gin

ho - ly and mild;_____ Sent from the high - -

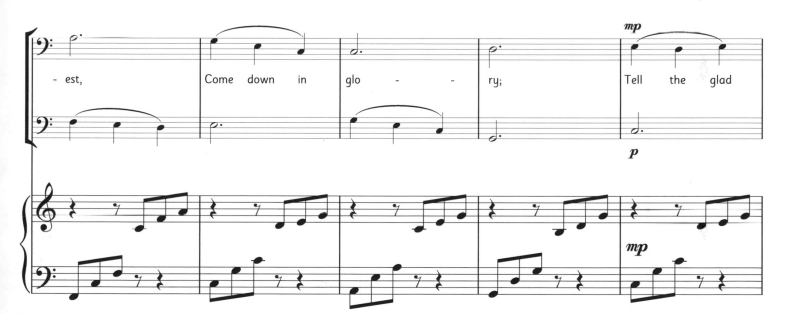

- est, Come down in glo - - ry; Tell the glad

sto - - ry, Wel - come the child._____

28. Jingle, bells

J. Pierpont (1822–93)

Happily ♪ = 144, swing

Jin - gle, bells,   jin - gle, bells,   jin - gle all   the way;

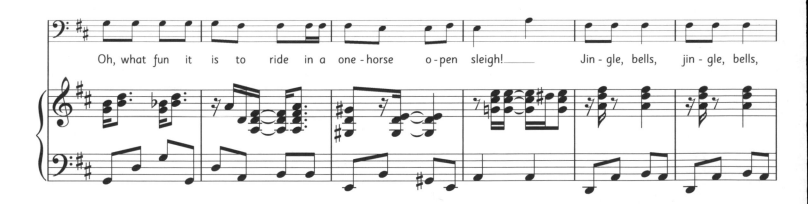

Oh, what fun it   is to   ride in a one - horse   o - pen sleigh!_____   Jin - gle, bells,   jin - gle, bells,

jin - gle all   the way;   Oh, what fun it   is to   ride   in a one - horse o - pen sleigh!

29. Mary had a baby

American trad.

30. Christmas Calypso

Kathy & David Blackwell

So dance the Christ-mas Ca-lyp-so in the sun, Je-sus is born for ev-'ry-one; Sing out with joy and

Fine

stamp your feet,____ move to the ca - lyp - so beat!____

mf

Way back in Beth - le - hem,____ in a sim - ple sta - ble,

mf

D.%. al Fine

Je - sus, that ba - by boy,____ came to save us all! So dance the

31. Hogmanay Reel

Kathy & David Blackwell

With energy ♩ = 100

32. Auld Lang Syne

With a wee dram! ♩ = 72

Scottish trad.

Should auld ac-quain-tance be for-got, and__ nev-er brought to mind? Should auld ac-quain-tance be for-got, for the sake of auld lang syne? For auld____ lang____ syne, my dear, for auld____ lang____ syne; We'll tak' a cup o' kind-ness yet, for the sake of auld lang syne.

Cello Time Christmas
piano accompaniment book

Cello Time is a great series for young cellists. Packed with lively original tunes, easy duets, and traditional pieces, the books are carefully paced and organized to build confidence every step of the way. With plenty of entertaining illustrations and audio to play along to, with **Cello Time** it really is fun to play!

Cello Time
by Kathy and David Blackwell

Cello Time Joggers
(a first book of very easy pieces)

cello book with audio
piano accompaniment book

Cello Time Runners
(a second book of easy pieces)

cello book with audio
piano accompaniment book

Cello Time Sprinters
(a third book of pieces)

cello book with audio
piano accompaniment book

Cello Time Christmas
(a stockingful of 32 easy pieces)

cello book with audio
piano accompaniment book

Cover illustration by Alan Rowe

OXFORD
UNIVERSITY PRESS

www.oup.com

ISBN 978-0-19-337225-2

9 780193 372252